B

by Sue Harrison and Dennis Yardley

Published by Newcastle upon Tyne
City Libraries and Arts

ACKNOWLEDGEMENTS:

Photograph 5 copyright Newcastle Chronicle and Journal Ltd
Photograph 17 copyright Newcastle City Engineers

Published by Newcastle upon Tyne City Libraries and Arts, 1990.

ISBN 0902653 79 2

INTRODUCTION

other Newcastle community
s experienced such rapid growth
r undergone such profound
ange over the years as Byker.

e original 'township of Byker'
nsisted of Byker Village and the
ighbouring villages of St Peter's,
Anthony's, Dent's Hole and Ouseburn.
om the mid-sixteenth century the
id process of industrialisation gained
othold mainly in the Ouseburn and
Peter's areas while Byker Village
elf retained an unspoilt rural
aracter, being completely surrounded
acres of fields. Industrial expansion
the area stemmed from the growth
the coal trade on the Tyne. The glass
dustry thrived during the nineteenth
ntury. This period also saw the
pansion of shipbuilding at St Peter's
d lead works, flint mills and potteries
the Ouseburn Valley. Maling Pottery
particular established a worldwide
putation for it's products.

ch rapid industrial development lead
an increase in population from 3254
1801 to 7040 in 1851. In 1835
wcastle extended it's boundaries to
lude Byker Township. The Newcastle
North Shields railway was opened in
1839 and was followed in 1879 by the
Riverside branch line. Communications
were given a further boost in 1878 with
the opening of Byker Bridge and the
development of other routes in and
around the area. Byker Township had
undergone a remarkable transformation
from rural community to a bustling
suburb of Newcastle. It ceased to exist
as an administrative unit in 1917 when
it was divided into the St Anthony's, St
Lawrence and Byker Wards.

The Lawson family, who had owned
most of Byker since 1543 sold an area
of land for housing development.
Byker's terraced streets were built in a
grid pattern sloping north-south
towards the river and east-west towards
the Ouseburn. This is the Byker so well
remembered – sloping cobbled streets,
back lanes and corner shops. Larger
shopping areas developed on Raby
Street, Brinkburn Street and Shields
Road, the latter becoming an important
shopping centre for the entire East-end
of Newcastle.

When it was decided to re-develop
Byker in the sixties, one of the main
objectives put forward was that the
strong social links with the community
should be retained. The outline
proposals in the 1968 report produced
by the City's Planning Officer and
Housing Architect also drew attention
to the location of a proposed motorway,
and the need for a solid line of
development to screen the new
housing areas from the the noise that it
would generate. 1300 homes were
demolished in the area behind Shields
Road to make way for the new road
and the Byker Wall came into being as
the architectural showpiece of the new
Byker – the motorway however, is only
now being built.

Change in Byker has been radical, but
some remnants of the old Byker remain
– some pubs, churches and Shipley
Street Baths. The photographs in this
booklet have been selected to rekindle
memories of Byker as it used to be.

1. BYKER BRIDGE
Byker Bridge cost £50,000 to build and was opened on 19 October 1878. Originally a toll-bridge, it was purchased by the City Council in 1890 for the sum of £107,500, although the toll was not lifted until 1895.

2. AVONDALE ROAD
This view of Avondale Road dates back to 1968 – prior to demolition for the re-development. This was a typical Byker view showing the terraced housing and steep streets. Avondale Road sloped down towards Raby Street, and beyond, in the centre is Raby Street School. This panoramic view shows the Tyne Bridge in the distance.

3. CLIFFORD STREET 1919
Street parties were held throughout the city to mark the end of World War I – Byker was no
exception. This photograph shows the residents of Clifford Street holding their celebration in 1919.

4. ST SILAS' CHURCH

St Silas' was built in 1886 with funds raised from an appeal launched by Newcastle's first bishop, Ernest Wilberforce, grandson of the anti-slavery campaigner. This photograph dates from about 1912, and shows the west end of the church.

5. BLACK'S REGAL 1934
The Regal was the second of three large cinemas, all of this name, built in the North East by Alfred Black: the others were in Sunderland (1932) and Gateshead (1937). The Byker Black's Regal was opened on 3 September 1934 with the William Powell – Bette Davis film 'Fashions of 1934'. The cinema seated 1120 in the stalls and 525 in the circle. The foyers were lavishly finished in walnut panels and copper. In 1955 the cinema became the Odeon, and it closed in 1972, being demolished in 1986–87.

6. AERIAL VIEW OF PARRISH'S
An aerial view showing Parrish's Department Store in the foreground. John Thomas Parrish began the business by opening a small shop at 10 Shields Road in 1875. By the 1880's it had expanded and moved to the site shown here at 166 Shields Road. Behind Parrish's on Brinkburn Street stands the former Brinkburn Cinema, which was at one time owned by Tyne Picture Houses, who also owned the Apollo, Shields Road.

7. NEWCASTLE CORPORATION TRAMWAYS STAFF
Newcastle tramway platform and maintenance staff pose at Byker Depot in front of a double-decker
tram in the 1920's.

8. GLASSHOUSE BRIDGES
This photograph, taken from the mouth of the River Ouseburn, shows the two Glasshouse Bridges and the Ship Inn. The nearer bridge dates from 1669, when Thomas Wrangham, a shipbuilder, replaced the previous wooden structure. May 1878 saw the opening of the larger bridge in the distance, constructed at a cost of £14,000.

9. SHIELDS ROAD 1897
This photograph was taken from the part of Shields Road which was known as Byker Hill. The Blue Bell Hotel can be seen on the left, complete with turrets which were later removed. Also featured are the old public conveniences which were positioned in the middle of Shields Road. Behind these can be seen a shop at 294 Shields Road belonging to J Davidson, a Corn Dealer.

10. HEADLAM STREET POLICE STATION

The 'new' East End Police and Fire Station was opened in July 1903 by the wife of Councillor Fred Elliott. Designed by Messrs Cackett and Burns Dick of Grainger Street. The building was in three sections: Fire Station, Police Station, and Police Inspector's House, with the main entrance to each in Headlam Street. The Fire Station closed in 1969, and the Police Station moved to Clifford Street on 6 January 1975. The old Headlam Street building was finally demolished three years later.

11. SHIELDS ROAD 1909
This illustration of Shields Road is dated about 1909. The centre trampoles were removed after World War I due to increased traffic, and were replaced with pavement mounted poles. Some of the shops in this photograph include Gilbert Foggin's Fishmongers; Public Benefit Boot Co Ltd and a drapers called Teago's.

12. NEW HAWK INN
One of Byker Bank's most famous pubs was built in the early 1880's as a free house. This photograph shows landlord Bob Gray standing at the back, wearing a white apron. The lady on the right is Liz Docherty who later took over the Locomotive in St Peter's. Bob Gray was a champion sculler on the Tyne, and in his later years was referee for the river races which took place from Hawthorn Leslie's, up to Scotswood.

13. OUSEBURN ROAD 1960
This photograph taken about 1960 shows the Flint Mill Cottages and the Ouseburn Cottages on Ouseburn Road. The scene is framed by the Ouseburn Viaduct which was built in 1839 – in the distance are the arches of Byker Bridge. The foreground shows the River Ouseburn exiting from the culvert which was built in 1906.

14. GRAND THEATRE

The Grand Theatre opened on July 27 1896 with a performance of 'The Taming of the Shrew'. During its existence it operated as a music hall, variety theatre, cinema, and finally as a venue for touring and resident revue. It closed on 21 August 1954 with a performance of 'Night Must Fall' by the Talent Players.

15. THE DEAD HOUSE

The Dead House was the city mortuary in the late 19th century. It was located at the 'Mushroom' boat landing near Spillers Mill – named after the 'Mushroom Inn', one of the last of the old riverside inns.

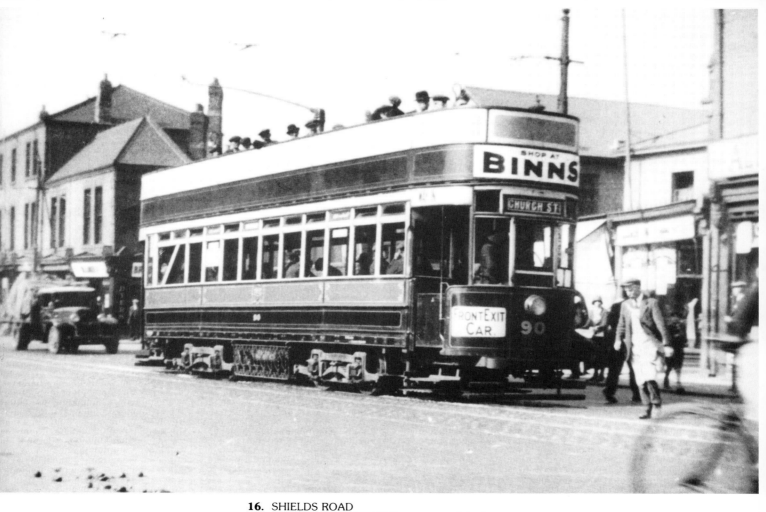

16. SHIELDS ROAD
Shields Road in the 1930's sees one of the largest trams in Britain – Newcastle F Class No. 90,
bound for Church Street, Walker, on a route converted to trolleybuses in 1937.

17. C T MALING AND SONS LTD
Malings were one of the largest producers of ceramics in the late 19th/early 20th century. The Ford (B) Pottery was completed in 1878 at a cost of £100,000. The buildings covered an area of 6½ acres and it was reputedly the largest pottery in Britain. Unlike most previous potteries, all the manufacturing processes were carried out under one roof.

18. ST PETER'S SCHOOL 1927/28

St Peter's was one of the first board schools provided by Newcastle School Board. Opened on July 22 1872 under its original name of St Lawrence's, the school moved to its permanent site at St Peter's in 1876. In 1926/27 the school catered for 1106 pupils. Miss E Watson became head of the junior section in 1927. Pupils had to suffer the dreadful smells emanating from a local glue factory.

19. RABY STREET

Old Byker meets new – a view contrasting the old Byker with the new. The Byker wall looks down on the terraced houses of Raby Street. Built originally as an effective sound barrier against noise from the proposed motorway, the Byker Wall is the dominant architectural feature of the redeveloped Byker.

20. BYKER VILLAGE 1925

The spire on the left of the picture belongs to St Michael's Church which was consecrated in 1862. The Church and its original vicarage still stand today – the old vicarage is now named David Grieve House and is the home of the Newcastle Battalion of the Boy's Brigade. The house on the right of the photograph stands today on what is now Welbeck Road. Much of the land here was owned by the Lawson family who lived at Byker Hall which was situated to the south of the village.